General information

You will require the following equipment

Blunt cocktail sticks
(cut one end off and sn

1. Dogbone tool.
2. Dresden tool.
3. Leicester tool (wood

1

2

3

Not actual size

Palette knife, egg white, cornflour, non-stick board and rolling pin, man-made sponge (foam), selection of paint brushes — sable — suggested Nos. 2 and 4, and cheap brush, No. 4. Use the cheap brush when applying the egg white or gum arabic solution. All brushes should be well washed after use.

Fine pointed scissors.
Tweezers.
Selection of different gauge wires, such as 24, 26, 28, 30 and 32.
Stretch flower tapes, especially light green, moss green and white.
Selection of droplet colours and dusting powders.
Paint palette.
Trex (white vegetable fat).

When working, keep the cut-out shape on the edge of the board, and the board on the edge of the table. This will give you the best angle for your cocktail stick. Keep remainder of the paste under cover at all times as it dries very quickly. Once the shape required has been cut out, thin down the paste even more by rocking the cocktail stick from the centre to one side of the petal, and then back to the centre and out to the other side. One hand guides the cocktail stick while the other hand applies the pressure, which should vary according to how much you wish the shape to alter. This will also texture the paste. In most instances the outside edge is expanded by up to three times the original size. This very thin paste can then be peeled from the board. The whole petal shape is spread so that it is translucent.

Sometimes paste is only thinned on the outer edge, as with poppies, nasturtiums, lilies, orchids etc. (any large petalled flower or leaf).

Fixing flowers on wires

Hold wire between thumb and third finger, which will then enable you to use your other thumb and the index fingers of both hands. By turning the wire you can pinch the paste into place with the two fingers and thumb. This technique is also useful when removing surplus paste from the underside of a flower, or modelling and neatening the general shape.

Flowers made from a long cone

When a long cone of paste is on a wire, as with the honeysuckle, summer and winter jasmine, petunias etc., it can be difficult to give a neat finish to the thin end if the paste has started to dry. Flatten the paste between your thumb and index finger, and then with your thumbnail take off the paste that does not touch the wire. Then apply pressure a couple of times with your two index fingers and thumb.

Don't forget, there will be a big difference in the final shaping of a flower, depending on whether the cone shape used is short and wide, or long with a narrow end.

Leaves and large petals

Use 30 gauge wire for small leaves and 26 or 28 gauge for the larger ones. Form a sausage of paste, dip the wire in egg white and then push through the dry end, until the wet end is inside the paste. With the wire away from you, roll this shape on the palm of your hand until it comes to a fine point at both ends. With the larger pieces of paste, use three fingers to do this rolling, exerting slightly more pressure at either end. Lay the wire plus paste on to a lightly greased board, and keep pressing your palette knife on to the shape until it is well flattened. Using your Leicester tool, thin down the paste either side of the wire. Once again press your palette knife gently over the wire. This may show up a thickness of paste which you can then thin down. The paste should now be stuck to the board, and you can then cut out the shape required. Remember that the wire should extend into the leaf shape about one third of the overall length.

Lift leaf (or petal) shape carefully from the board with your palette knife from the wire end, and turn over. The underside will now be the surface for the finished shape. Place on foam and indent the main vein with your palette knife. Stand leaves (or petals) in a piece of polystyrene to dry.

Note: The base of the leaf shape does not necessarily have to be cut from the edge of the paste (wire end).

Finish of leaves

EITHER dust and then steam: Push leaf wires into polystyrene, about five at a time, boil a kettle and then pass the leaves backwards and forwards through the steam, possibly about three or four times, until they just start to shine. With the fine end of a cocktail stick you can then remove the dusting colour where the veins are.

OR paint the upper surface with droplet colour and gum arabic solution. While still wet, remove paint with the fine end of your cocktail stick where the veins are, continually cleaning the point as you work. When the leaves are nearly dry you may like to dust the edges with another colour, such as pink, red, yellow or brown.

Gum arabic solution

Use one part gum arabic to three parts triple strength rose water, orange water, or boiled water. (Boiled water will not give you such a long shelf life as the other two.)

Variety in leaf shape

Cutters are made for many different leaf shapes that are constantly being used, such as holly, ivy, oak and chrysanthemum, but sometimes an unusual leaf is needed.

Cut out a sheet of fairly thin card, (such as is used for cereal packets) and lay strips of double sided tape edge to edge, from top to bottom of the cardboard, so it is completely covered. Remove covering of tape. Take a fresh leaf, and carefully press this into the sticky surface, making sure it is completely flat. On a cutting mat, or very thick cardboard, carefully cut away the surplus card, so that only the leaf remains with the card backing.

Rose

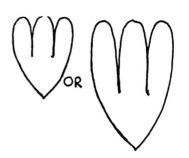

Requirements

2 x 24 gauge wires taped together and hooked for each flower. Use up old paste when making centres for your roses.

1. Dip a hooked 24 gauge wire in egg white, and fix into a blob of paste that is quite pointed. The size should be within the length of the petal part of the shape.

   Allow to dry at least overnight.

2. *See explanation of using two different coloured pastes alongside rose picture.* Roll out the two pastes, then put one on top of the other and roll again. Cut out five of the shape (one extra in case of an accident). Keeping the remainder under cover, take one shape and place it on the edge of a lightly greased board. Starting on the left hand side (if you are right handed), use the blunt end of your cocktail stick, and start from the centre and thin down the paste with a rocking action. Go back to the centre and repeat out to the other side. Control the pressure on your cocktail stick with the index finger of your other hand. The idea is to create the shape of the conventional rose petal, which by this time should be two to three times the original size. Flick this over and work the second petal in the same way, then the third petal. Grease the board again after each shape has been worked.

3. Dip dried centre in the egg white.

   WITH EVERY SHAPE paint egg white on the bottom triangle as well as the petals, even though it is eventually removed.

I usually work with two different coloured pastes, one on top of the other then rolled together, with generally the darker one underneath. Even when making a white rose it is better to have slightly coloured paste underneath as it gives a good shaded effect. There is no need to texture the petals as the method of using your cocktail stick will do this, and dusting the finished flower will not be necessary. The petals will be spiralled automatically as you work, and with only four of the shapes a complete rose can be made.

If many roses are required of the same colour, make up two large lumps of the differently coloured paste and just take enough to make one rose at a time. The surplus paste, when kneaded, will make flowers that will blend well with the original choice. It is perhaps best to use cream or pale yellow as the paler colour when using up the surplus kneaded paste.

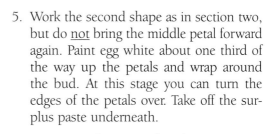

4. Only with this first shape, bring the middle petal forward, completely paint it with egg white, and wrap it around the 'rose centre' very tightly. Paint the egg white almost to the top of the remaining two petals and stick the right hand one at the back and bring the left hand one forward and stick that to the front. Now wrap these two around. They should tuck inside each other. Take off surplus paste underneath. If you put a calyx on at this stage, it can serve as a tight bud.

5. Work the second shape as in section two, but do <u>not</u> bring the middle petal forward again. Paint egg white about one third of the way up the petals and wrap around the bud. At this stage you can turn the edges of the petals over. Take off the surplus paste underneath.

6. Repeat on shape number three, paint on egg white, wrap round flowerhead and turn down petals. This should go roughly three quarters of the way round the flower.

7. Cut one petal off the last shape. Work and paint with egg white as before, and place in the gap. Trim away the surplus paste from the last two shapes.

8. Cut out calyx, curl sepals with dogbone tool on foam, paint with egg white, and position at the back of the rose. Form a small pea shape of the same green as the calyx, change this to an oval shape. Brush one end with egg white, and slide this up the wire to position it directly below the calyx.

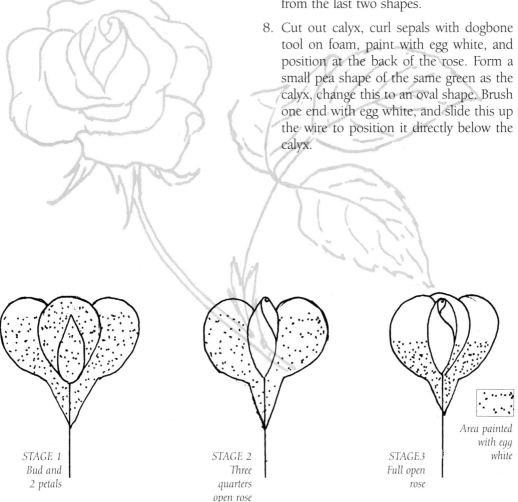

STAGE 1
Bud and
2 petals

STAGE 2
Three
quarters
open rose

STAGE3
Full open
rose

Area painted
with egg
white

Freesia

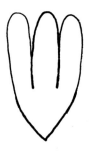

Requirements *24 and 28 gauge wire, cutter as shown, stamens and dusting powders.*

1. Tape three stamen threads to a 24 gauge wire, winding on enough tape to make a sausage shape. Make sure that the stamens are not longer than the petals.

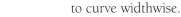

2. Separate stamens and dip in egg white, then in powder colour to match the finished flower, i.e. white pollen if white flower etc. An extra plain white stamen can be added as a pistil.

3. Roll out flower paste and cut out two shapes. Leaving one under cover, place the other on your hand and quickly soften edges with back of dogbone tool. Put shape back on the board, splay petals apart, and using the blunt end of a cocktail stick, apply pressure to the edge of the petals and roll outwards (leaving thicker paste in the middle). After all three petals have been thinned, indent each with a few lines and cup the ends with a balling tool. Press a dresden tool flat down each petal

to curve widthwise.

4. Paint egg white on triangular end and about quarter way up each petal.

5. Place prepared stamens on petal shape, with the sausage of tape just below the petals, and roll so the petals completely surround the centre. It is possibly easier to do the final positioning while standing up, so that the petals are pointing down all the time that you are working. If necessary, hang the flower upside down until dry. It is easier to fix on the second layer when the first shape is dry.

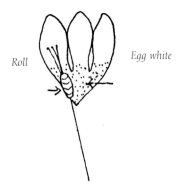

Roll *Egg white*

6. Work the second shape in the same way and paint with egg white.

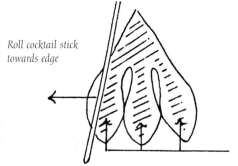

Roll cocktail stick towards edge

Leave paste thicker in the middle

Flowers are best made with a very pale cream paste, as the petals are often yellow at the base. The flowers are then best dusted as required when the flower is complete and dry. Try to have a good look at a real spray, as the way each flower head leads from the previous one is an essential part of the character of the whole flower spray.

7. Place the dried petals over the newly worked shape so that the petals are over a space. Roll the petals round and press firmly into place. Again, hang upside down, if necessary, until dry. Dust with appropriate colour.

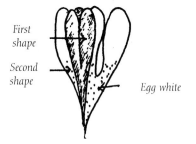

First shape

Second shape

Egg white

8. **Buds:** Colour some paste green, cream and green mixed, and some just cream. Buds change colour as they grow. Make a few very small plain green buds, then some a bit lighter and bigger, taking note from nature of the shaping, especially of the larger buds. For the bud that is about to open, form a round ended shape, put on a hooked wire and allow to dry overnight. Cover with one worked shape. With middle sized buds, form shape, indent deeply about 3 times with your palette knife and gently roll on your hand. Put onto hooked wire.

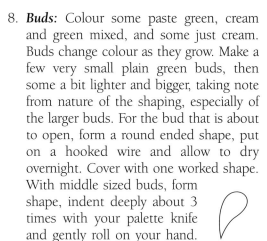

9. **Calyx:** With a slightly darker green than the smallest buds, make a cone shape. Open this up with the point of a cocktail stick and then, with the blunt end, roll round inside until you have a thin, hollow cone. Cut out two wide 'V' shapes and the calyx will now resemble a bird's open beak. Thin cut edge again with cocktail stick. Paint a small amount of egg white inside and slip up wire to base of flower. Vary the size of calyx according to the size of the bud or flower. The smallest buds will be nearly covered by the calyx.

10. Using tweezers, position two tiny buds next to each other, tape together and then add any extra buds, getting larger each time until full flower, or flowers, are added to complete the spray. When the last flower is added the direction of the stalk usually changes.

When these are used in a group of other flowers, as in a formal spray, it is sometimes advisable and easier to use three buds taped together, and use the open flowers on their own.

Marguerite

and similar shaped flowers

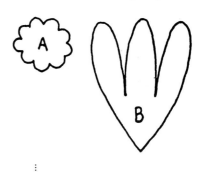

Requirements *Two 24 gauge wires, about 3½" long, for each flower. Circle of foil and small piece of Blu-tack.*

1. Cut two equal lengths of 24 gauge wire, tape them together, and hook one end.

2. Form a slightly flattened cone of green paste, cut out shape 'A', turn it over, slightly hollow out and thin down edges. Make sure you leave a thickness of paste at the bottom of the 'bowl'. On the rounded side of the calyx you can make some 'V' shaped cuts, starting from the centre and working out towards the edge. Gently press these points back in place. Dip hook in egg white and pull through so that the end is well embedded in the paste. Allow to dry overnight.

3. Cut out a circle of foil approximately 3" across. Push this up behind the dried calyx and put a roll of Blu-tack directly behind to keep it in place.

4. For a single layer of petals, cut out three of shape 'B'. Put two shapes under cover and just work on one at a time. Taking one shape, press hard on the sides of the paste with the back of your dogbone tool in order to soften the edges. Cut down through the centre of each petal to its base. On a well-greased board, work the edges of the petals with a blunt cocktail stick, giving extra attention to the inner cut edge, which is pointed at one side. When pressure is applied evenly to this area the petal will quickly become

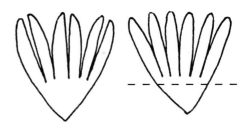

Cocktail stick "shoulder"

rounded. It may be easier to use the 'shoulder' of your cocktail stick on the inside edge of the petals.

5. Lay the shape on a board and cut off bottom triangle about half way up and then cut out small 'V' shapes across the width, probably three or four times. Put the shape on a greased part of the board and push the bottom outside edges together so that the cut 'V' shapes virtually join up together again. This will bring the whole shape into more of a curve.

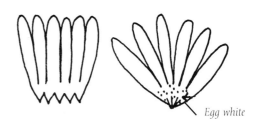

Egg white

Hopefully, this is a much easier way of making this type of flower. One or two layers of petals can be made.

6. Paint egg white on roughly one third of the surface of the dried calyx, and place the prepared petals on this part. Make sure that the base of the petals is inside the rim of the calyx. Each shape should make one third of the whole flower.

7. Repeat with two other shapes. You could now cut out another three shapes if a fuller effect is required. Do not put these directly on top of the previous shapes, try to alternate them.

8. For the yellow centre, take a rough measurement of the area in the centre to be covered. (I usually do this with my tweezers.) Form a slightly domed shape of mid-green paste to the size needed. Rough up the surface with the points of your tweezers (held closed), allow to dry a little and either dust with bright yellow powder or paint with gum arabic, allow to become 'tacky' and then dust. Mix some icing glue (flower paste and egg white mixed together to look like stiff royal icing). Put a small amount of glue in the prepared centre (use an old cocktail stick for this). Push the pointed end of your cocktail stick into the centre in order to lift it away from the flower, and blow off any surplus powder. Now pick up the yellow centre on your palette knife and carefully position it in the middle of the flower, pressing it gently into place with another cocktail stick.

Leaves

The leaves can vary quite a bit in shape and colour, but I have copied the ones in my garden, which are very dark green. This helps to show up the flowers and gives good variation of foliage in the arrangement.

Form a sausage of green paste, dip 28 gauge green wire in egg white, pull through, roll on palm of hand, giving extra pressure to either end. This will really embed the wire into the paste. Flatten paste with palette knife on a lightly greased board and then roll out either side until fairly thin. Lift off the board, find out if the wire is not too far in (pull out gently if necessary). Put back on greased board and then thin again until paste is stuck down. Cut into the edge at regular intervals, as in the diagram.

Carnation (new)

Requirements

For each flower you will need two 26 gauge light green wires taped together with half width white stretch tape. Pale blue/green paste for leaves and calyx and choice of colour for flower — anything in the yellow or pink range, as well as white, cream and red. Also 30 gauge white wire for leaves.

1. For the calyx, form a cone of paste about ³/₄" long, pointed at one end and slightly rounded at the other. Hollow out the narrow end about half way down. Thin down rim and cut out five 'V' shapes. Dip hooked wires in egg white and pull through until well embedded in the paste. At the stem end make two cuts, opposite each other, by sliding the blades of the scissors over the paste until they are nearly together, and then make a little snip. Repeat in between but lower down. Push points back into calyx so they are flush with the surface.

2. Roll out paste fairly thin, and cut out at least seven shapes. Work one shape at a time. Soften the edges quickly with the back of a dogbone tool. Make small cuts on the ends of each petal. Working on a greased board, roll out each petal — the complete petal length, working from the centre out until it has at least doubled in size. Place shape on foam and gently curve the ends with a small balling tool.

3. Cut out a 'V' shape from base and then push sides towards the centre until it is all one piece again. Using the pointed end of the cocktail stick pressed into the petals, gather them together and then shear away any surplus paste from the bottom part of the shape.

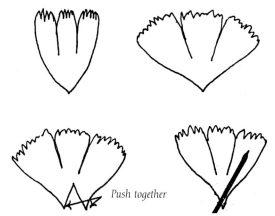

Push together

Use cocktail stick to push all 3 petals together

4. Paint egg white in calyx and put shape in so that the three petals hang over the edge. Press into place with blunt end of cocktail stick. Continue with next two shapes in the same way, pulling some petals up and some down. Try and leave a little space in between so you can see where to place the next three shapes. Take out any surplus paste in the calyx as you work.

5. With the next row, position the next three shapes so that they alternate with the previous ones, again arranging the petals in a 'free' manner.

6. Taking the last shape, prepare it in the same way. Paint egg white along the base of the petals and then roll it up. Trim off quite a bit of the pointed part at the base, paint egg white in the centre of the flower and put in the last shape; using the pointed end of your cocktail stick to pick it up and push it into place. Twist the stick to remove it, hopefully leaving the petals at the same height as the six already in position.

Buds

1. Tape together two 28 gauge light green wires, about 2" long, with half width white tape and hook one end.

2. Form pointed cone, snip rounded base in the same way as the calyx of the open flower. Dip wire in egg white, pull through until hook is embedded in paste. Allow to dry and then dust a little yellow on the pointed tip.

Leaves

1. Make a small sausage of the blue/green paste. Cut a 2" length of 30 gauge white wire, dip in egg white, pull wire through until wet end is well into the paste, roll the full length on the palm of your hand so that it is pointed at both ends.

2. Grease the board, lay the paste down with the wire pointing away from you and flatten with a palette knife. Roll out paste until very thin either side of the wire, making sure the paste is really well stuck to the board, and then cut a very narrow shape approximately two inches long. Place on foam and indent main vein by pressing down with your palette knife along the full length. Make two of these leaves, curl each one, which are then positioned either side of the stem at the junction of a bud and flower. If you wish to curl these leaves it may be better to put them onto a 32 gauge wire and curl over your Leicester tool as soon as you have indented the main vein.

Carnation: General remarks

This method, hopefully, should enable you to make a daintier and more interesting flower than is achieved with the conventional way. Whether you know this flower as carnation, pink or dianthus, the range of colour is immense.

Open Rose: General remarks

This is possibly a daintier type of rose for cake decoration. It is based on the patio rose variety or the cottage rambler. The paste for petals is thinned down with a blunt cocktail stick while stuck to a lightly greased board. This is done with a rocking action, slightly lifting the cocktail stick before positioning it each time. **At no time is the cocktail stick just rolled backwards and forwards in the middle of the petal.** This will only leave a ridge of thick paste on the edges.

Open rose

Requirements

24 gauge green wires for flowers.

28 or 30 gauge light green wires for leaves.

30 gauge white wire for securing stamens.

Cream cotton (must be cotton if you wish to stiffen stamens).

1. Preparation of the stamens: Leaving a length of cotton free, wind the cotton round your finger about twenty times and finish with another length free. Slip the loop of cotton off your finger and push through a 2" length of 30 gauge white wire. Twist the wire tightly. Push another length through on the opposite side; twist tightly as before. With the free ends of cotton, tie round securely just above where the wire went through. This will make two centres. Cut loop in half.

2. Tape the stamen wire to a 3" length of 24 gauge wire and add more tape at the base of the stamens to keep them upright. If you wish to stiffen the cotton, dip it in egg white and leave to dry overnight. Form a tiny round shaped piece of light green paste. Open up the centre of the cotton (I usually do this with the blunt end of a cocktail stick), paint in some egg white and then push in the little piece of green paste. Paint the ends of the stamens with egg white and dip in yellow dusting powder. Add a little brown powder afterwards if the rose is to be fully open.

3. Roll out the paste and cut out about six or seven pieces and keep them well covered. Lightly grease the board and, taking one shape at a time, put it on the edge of the board. Work the left hand part first (if you are right handed), thinning down by using your cocktail stick. Make sure the paste is stuck to the board. Work out from the centre to the left, and then back to the centre and out to the right hand side, until a rose petal shape is achieved. Turn this petal over and work the next two petals in the same way. They should now overlap each other. The bottom 'V' shape should not be thinned down.

4. Place the petals on foam and, with your dresden tool, curl the petals inwards by stroking the paste from the edge, at the same time slightly twisting the tool, which should make the petals curl over. This is better than balling the edge if you can manage it as it doesn't crack the back surface of the petals.

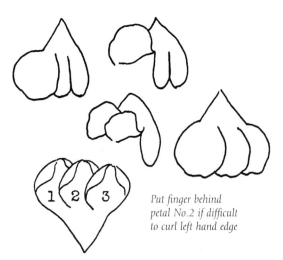

Put finger behind petal No.2 if difficult to curl left hand edge

16

5. Paint egg white on to the bottom triangle and up about one third of each petal. Wrap shape around stamens, making sure that the bottom of the petals comes below the base of the stamens. Peel off the surplus paste underneath the flower.

6. Work the next shape in the same way, paint on egg white as before. This will form part of the next layer. Try to see that one petal does not go directly behind another. Curl subsequent petals from the back so that they curl downwards. Keep taking off surplus paste when you have put on about two shapes. You will probably only need five or six shapes to complete the flower.

7. Check on the nearly completed flower, you may need to add a single petal occasionally. (Cut out shape shown right and cut one petal off, and work in the same way.)

8. Cut out calyx from thin paste. Many varieties of rose (not all) have little pieces sticking out from the edges of the sepals. Curve calyx on foam and paint with egg white and position behind flower. Put small ball of paste behind calyx.

Leaves

Cut a 2" length of 28 or 30 gauge light green wire for each leaf. Using a mid-tone green paste, roll out a sausage shape. Dip wire in egg white and push through the dry end until wet end is inside the paste. Put this on the palm of your hand, wire away from you, and roll with three fingers until the paste is pointed at both ends.

Lay wire and paste on a lightly greased board (use white vegetable fat such as Trex) and press down on paste with a palette knife several times. With your palette knife lift up the wire and this will show you where the end of the wire is. The wire should only come into the finished leaf shape by about one third of the length. Roll out the paste *either side of the wire* and again press very gently with your palette knife over the wire. this can show up a thickness of paste which can then be rolled away. The paste should now be well stuck to the board. Cut out the required shape with your craft knife. Using about a one inch length of the serrated metal from the side of a cling film box, press and pull away from the edge. Do not serrate the bottom curve.

Lift the paste off the board with your palette knife, turn it over.

Place leaf on foam and press down on centre vein with your palette knife. Just press down and then lift off. Do not move the knife with any other movement than down then up, otherwise the leaf will be cut. The leaves come in groups of three (just behind flower-head) and five, with the largest at the top getting progressively smaller as you go down the complete leaf. If you have time, put on a stipule at the base of each complete leaf. This is a triangular shaped green structure with a small "v" shape cut out of the wider end, This should be made of extremely thin paste. Fix with egg white on top of wire where it joins the main stem.

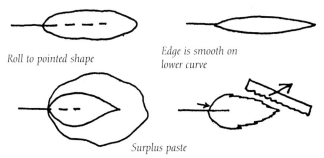

Roll to pointed shape

Edge is smooth on lower curve

Surplus paste

Cornflower

Requirements *Two 26 gauge wires, taped together and hooked for each flower. Thick black stamen threads. Mauve/violet paste for centre, blue paste for petals. Make cone as in Section 1 below at least one day before.*

1. Form a cone about quarter of an inch in length and slightly less than quarter of an inch across the flat top. Dip the hooked wire in the egg white and pull through the cone, push paste over the hole this has created. With sharp pointed scissors, cut the top surface all over, especially all round the edge. Push in about five short pieces of black stamen thread. Put on one side and allow to dry, preferably overnight.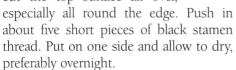

2. Roll out blue paste and cut out about eight shapes. This is an approximate number as it will depend on the size of your cone and how well you bunch the petals. Work one shape at a time, starting with the left hand petal if you are right handed. Place shape on the edge of a slightly greased board. Using your cocktail stick spread the paste from the centre out one way and then out the other way to form a triangular shape. (You may need to change the direction of your cocktail stick.) The paste should now be stuck to the board and this will enable you to cut out deep 'V' shapes all along the edge of the petal. For extra shaping place 'shoulder' of pointed end of the cocktail stick on the points, one at a time, and rock the stick from side to side. This will change the shape from a V to a wishbone curve.

Turn the petal over and work middle one in the same way, and then the last one. Place the shape on to a firm pad or hard part of the palm of your hand, position 'shoulder' of cocktail stick at the base of the petal, tipping it downwards very slightly, and rock. This action should bring the sides up and thus form a 'floret'. Repeat this action on the other two petals.

3. Cut out a 'V' shape from the base and then press sides towards the centre, on a lightly greased board, until it is all one piece again. Using the pointed end of the cocktail stick pressed into the petals, gather them together, squash the paste at the base and then shear away any surplus from the bottom part of the shape.

4. Paint egg white on to the paste below the petals and place in position on the side of the dried cone. When adding subsequent petals slightly overlap the previous one.

Although these flowers come in many colours, most people think of them as blue. Each flower is actually made up of many florets, but these are time-consuming to make, so this method is to create an impression of the flower rather than give an accurate copy. Keep the centre cone small.

5. Continue working each shape in the same way until the whole flower is completed. It could be that an extra few shapes might be needed if a fuller flower is required.

6. **Calyx:** Form quite a rounded cone shape — approximate size as shown. Using pointed end of cocktail stick, hollow out narrow end and then cut out rough- ly five 'V' shapes round the rim. (You can, at this stage, cut 'V' shapes on the calyx with your scissors, or marks can be made with black colour when the calyx is in place and dry). Paint egg white in the cavity of the calyx and pull the flower through into position.

7. When dry, dust with darker blue and/or violet colouring.

8. The leaves tend to be short and narrow. Cut 2in lengths of 30 gauge light green wire. Make sausage of light green paste, dip wire in egg white and push through paste until the end that has been dipped is about in the middle. Roll paste on the palm of your hand, with the wire pointing away from you, and work until it is cigar shaped. Grease board with Trex and lay paste on it. Flatten with a palette knife and then roll out either side until the paste is extremely thin. Again, gently flatten the paste over the wire and roll away the thickness that may show up. Cut to required shape, i.e. about $\frac{1}{4}$" wide and about $1"/1\frac{1}{2}"$ long. Lift off board careful- ly, turn paste over, place on foam and indent main vein with side of palette knife. Curve slightly and put on one side to dry. Make about three for each stem.

Anemone: General remarks

The number of petals varies quite considerably between the double and single varieties. I usually make the flowers in white and then dust with the required colour. The colour quite often fades to white near the stamens. The main colours are white, cream, red, purple, deep violet and dark blue.

Gerbera: General remarks

This is a very dramatic flower, with a strong colour range. When fresh, the petals tend to stand up in a fairly rigid manner.

Anemone

Requirements

Black thread for stamens. 30 gauge green wires for stamens. 28 gauge green wires for the leaves. Two 24 gauge green wires for each flower.

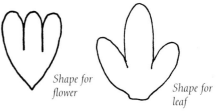

Shape for flower

Shape for leaf

1. Prepare stamens first by winding black cotton about thirty times round something like a pencil. Slide the loop off and push through a three inch length of 30 gauge wire. Twist wire underneath to secure thread. Tie a knot with the thread just above the wire. Roll an extra bit of tape round the base of the stamens and cut the loop to free the stamens. Open up the centre of the threads, paint in some egg white and put in a tiny cone of black paste.

   Tie just above wire

2. Roll out the white paste and cut out three to four shapes for each flower. Do not make the paste too thin. (Sometimes I put on a couple more petals — taken from one extra shape.)

3. Work the first shape. Starting with the left hand petal, if you are right handed, thin down the paste by rocking the cocktail stick from the centre out to the left hand outer edge, then back to the centre and thin out to the right hand side. The petal should now be a more rounded shape, at least twice the original size. Flick this one over and work the middle petal in the same way, then the third. All petals should now have thin paste, but the bottom 'triangle' should still be of the original thickness.

4. Curve all the petals on foam with your dogbone tool.

5. Paint egg white on the bottom triangle and wrap around the base of the stamens. Pinch paste into place by using your two index fingers and thumb and remove the

surplus paste from underneath. Decide now whether you want an open or partially closed flower and adjust the petals accordingly.

6. Work the next two shapes in exactly the same way, fixing each behind the first layer, trying to alternate the petals. You should end up with three petals round the stamens and six petals surrounding the centre. Allow the flower to dry and then dust.

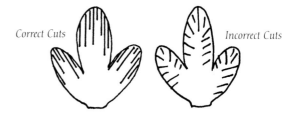

Correct Cuts

Incorrect Cuts

7. **Leaves:** Work one leaf at a time. Make a sausage of green paste. Roll out the paste really thinly on either side, leaving a thin ridge in the middle. Cut out shape 'B', lift the leaf off the board and cut each of the lobes many times with scissors, keeping the cuts in parallel lines. Put back on the lightly greased board and roll each of the 'fingers' with the blunt end of your cocktail stick. Dip a 2" length of 28 gauge wire into the egg white and then push into the ridge. Put leaf on to the foam and curve with the dogbone tool and then flick the 'fingers' (slightly twist). Make three leaves to go with each flower. When they are dry, brush edges with yellow and light brown powder colour and bend leaves to near right angles and place in position, about one inch behind the flowerhead, all at the same level.

Gerbera

Requirements

Six 24 gauge wires (cut two of the wires about quarter of an inch longer). Tape two together three times and then tape all together. The two slightly longer wires will be turned over for a hook. Paste colours: green, cream and colour of flower. Blu-tack and two layers of foil cut to make 4" diameter circles.

1. Hook the longer part of the wires. Form a fat cone of green paste about three quarters of an inch long. Open up the narrow end and hollow out, but make sure that there is a thickness at the base to take the hooked wires. Thin down rim until very fine and cut out many small 'V' shapes all the way round. Place the points of straight fine tweezers either side of the small cuts and gently squeeze down about an eighth of an inch, and repeat in between these down to the base. Try not to make the marks too regular or deep. *Allow to dry overnight.* Dip wires in egg white and push through.

2. Cut out circles of foil and pleat to make into a funnel shape and secure in place with Blu-tack directly between the calyx.

3. The petals are sometimes a lighter colour on the underside, and this can be achieved by rolling two colours of paste together, having the cream colour underneath. If you are not very quick at working, only roll out enough paste to cut out three shapes, so make sure you have two large lumps of paste and just take a small quantity from each at a time.

```
Section 2 .. last line
between should be below
```

4. Take one shape and keep the rest under cover. Place paste on your hand and quickly soften edges with the back of a dogbone tool. Cut each petal in half for the full length and thin down by laying the blunt cocktail stick the full length and gently pressing just on the edge. The inner cuts of each petal will need extra pressure so that round ended petals are achieved. Turn the paste over and either place on the edge of the palm of your hand or on one of the Cel Pads or Orchard Product Pads, and by placing your cocktail stick full length of the petal in the middle and gently rocking, the sides of the petals will curl upwards. Put the petals on your foam and gently curl the back of the ends of the petals with the small end of your dogbone tool. Make sure the cuts are the full length of the petals.

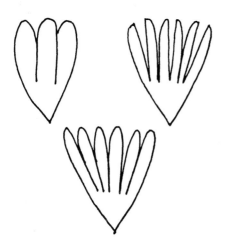

5. Turn paste back to the right side, cut off a small triangle from the base and then cut out three or four 'V' shapes. On a greased part of the board press the base together, which will then curve the outer edge of the petals overall. Brush back of the petals or calyx with egg white and lay petals in place, so that the base of the petals is on or below the rim of the calyx. This will be approximately one third of the first layer

of petals. When this layer is completed, dust with deeper colour.

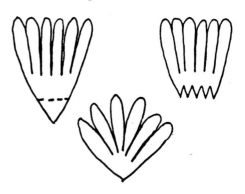

6. Complete about three layers making 2 with large cutter and 1 with small cutter, dusting on colour each time, but make sure the shapes of each are not directly over the previous ones, i.e. alternate them.

7. Cut out two small daisy shapes, still with the two layers of paste. Working on one shape at a time, halve each petal, thin down edges, curve petals inwards, paint back of shape with egg white and place in the centre of the flower, pushing well down. Work second shape in the same way. Not all varieties have these inner rows of petals.

8. Form a small cone, about quarter of an inch long and slightly smaller in diameter than the opening left in the centre of the flower. Cut this many times across the flat end of the cone, especially round the edge. If you can, thin down the cuts on the edge with the blunt end of your cocktail stick, so that they look like small petals. Paint the pointed end of the cone with egg white and push into the centre. When dry, touch surface of cone with white paste colour which has been tinged with yellow droplets.

9. The leaves tend to be broad, light green, and of an irregular shape. Flowers and leaves grow directly out of the ground.